Diminishing Resources
Water

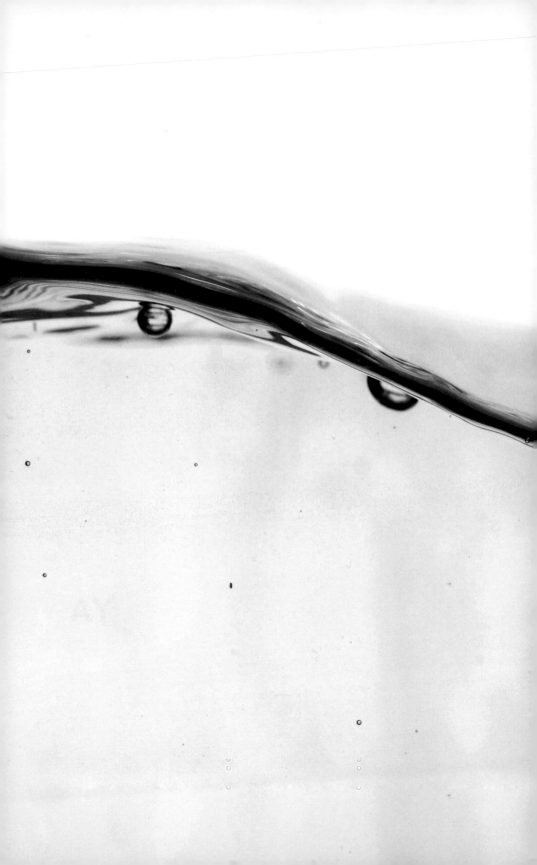

Diminishing Resources
Water

James G. Workman

MORGAN
REYNOLDS
P U B L I S H I N G

Greensboro, North Carolina

Diminishing Resources
SERIES

Soil | Forests | Water | Oil

Diminishing Resources: Water

Copyright © 2010 by Morgan Reynolds Publishing

Library of Congress Cataloging-in-Publication Data

Workman, James G.
  Diminishing resources. Water / by James Workman. -- 1st ed.
    p. cm.
  Includes bibliographical references and index.
  ISBN 978-1-59935-115-5 (alk. paper)
  1. Water-supply--History--Juvenile literature. 2. Water-supply--
Management--Juvenile literature. 3. Water-supply--Forecasting-
-Juvenile literature. 4. Water consumption--Juvenile literature. 5.
Droughts--Juvenile literature. I. Title.
  TD348.W67 2009
  363.6'1--dc22

                          2009028708

Printed in the United States of America
First Edition

To the thousands of nameless children who
die quietly each day from lack of clean water;
and to the thousands of nameless students who
try quietly each day to alter that needless fate

Contents

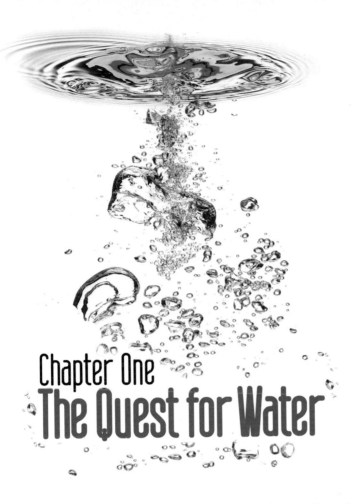

Chapter One
The Quest for Water

For anyone with money in Las Vegas, there is not much one is prohibited from doing. Overindulge at an all-you-can-eat buffet. Gamble around the clock on horses, slots, card tables, or roulette. Best of all, pay no income tax.

But try running a "water feature" at midday, or hosing down the sidewalk at full blast. The police will swarm out of nowhere, videotape the act, and issue a stiff fine. Water is the one thing Las Vegas does not have in abundance, and so its use has become the most tightly regulated activity in an otherwise free society. Unrestrained water use is closely monitored, frowned upon, and when possible, severely punished in Las Vegas.

Extravagant water features are the norm at Las Vegas resorts. Pictured here is the Bellagio Hotel's dancing fountains. Fountains and water features considered integral to the operation of a resort hotel are exempt from the city's water-use restrictions.

Some city leaders are trying to soften the edge of water restrictions wherever possible, sometimes in creative ways. One program offered to buy up the rights to lawns. Another project pays California to desalinate water at the coast, and then use a proportionate share of California's water from the Colorado River. But as Las Vegas grows, with new hook-ups to the water system every day, the city keeps reaching out farther and farther for more and more. It has to extend its intake pipe lower into the vanishing reservoir behind Hoover Dam. And by elbowing for more water in the region, it increasingly comes in conflict with neighboring states like Arizona and, especially, Utah.

In Las Vegas, an otherwise "anything goes," freewheeling city, water is the one exceptional big-government rule.

Few Americans can trace the source of their water beyond a pipe in the wall. Each day people wake up and turn a tap, start the laundry, run the dishwasher, take a shower, or flush the toilet. It's such a simple and reliable everyday act that few ponder how the water got there in the first place, or where it eventually goes.

People consist of 74 percent water, and can't exist without it. Water is the source of all food. It is also the source of most energy.

But many authorities now confess that they don't know where new water will come from, and where it should go. Water depletion afflicts not only the arid American West, but also the lush Southeast, and increasingly in thirty-six states across the country. And this situation is not unique to the United States. Today, 1.1 billion people lack access to water worldwide; 2,800 die each day from inadequate water; and 66 percent of the world will face water stress within the next fifteen years.

For most of human evolution, and for most of the world, access to water was never taken for granted. For billions of people, finding enough water remains a daily battle that can sometimes turn violent. Even the affluent world must struggle valiantly, and often fail spectacularly, in its constant quest to ensure there is enough water to quench all thirsts. But despite our advanced, booming, and globalized economy—indeed because of it—much of the United States is now facing the prospect of permanent drought, a man-made condition in which demand for water outstrips supply.

For decades America has been borrowing both against past water supplies and against future generations just to stay in place. The U.S. has led the world and fed the world. But with every crop grown and exported and every kilowatt generated and transferred, America has depleted water that we may never recover.

The potential for conflict over water depletion is real, at every level of society. It is no coincidence that the words *river* and *rival* share the same Latin root. Where other natural disasters unite society in a common effort of mutual cooperation, water scarcity breeds distrust. Drought has the negative tendency to turn us inward and against one another: your lawn vs your neighbor's pool, your city vs. rural farmers, local shopkeepers vs. multinational industries, Canada vs. U.S. vs. Mexico.

Scientists find it increasingly hard to define the deceptively simple term *drought*. The word goes beyond rigid notions of natural, hot, dry, cyclical episodes lasting a finite length of time. Drought is becoming recognized as a subjective, relative, economic, political, and man-made condition, and one that, given current trends, may not end at all.

A crowd of people in Meru, a town in Kenya near the northeastern slope of Mount Kenya, gathers around a tiny spring to collect water. Water scarcity has been an issue in Kenya for decades, and large numbers of women and children spend one-third of their day fetching clean water.

Drought can take place in a cool, dry era; but more importantly there is no longer a ceiling or end to what was once seen as cyclical self-regulating temperatures. Due to climate change, heat is rising a degree every decade throughout the world, and shows no sign of slowing.

Drought can even cripple landscapes that receive the same average rains and snowfall as in the past. Water supply shrinks even as demand expands, where populations have quadrupled or cities have increased ten- to twentyfold, or where the diets of stable but increasingly affluent economies consume four to forty times more water from the same finite sources.

Drought also comes as snowpack and glaciers melt faster and earlier from rising heat or falling dust. The same quantity of rain falls in sudden storms all at once, causing flash floods followed by dry skies. And what rain or snow does fall evaporates much faster under the heat, leaving less run-off in rivers and aquifers.

These three potent forces—global warming, decreasing supply from the resulting shocks, and escalating thirst of human populations—may combine all at once in the same place, as appears to be happening in the U.S. When that happens, what used to be short and cyclical dry spells grow long, and even permanent. Water depletion becomes not a temporary hardship but a perpetual affliction. This unnatural scenario may be described as a Perfect Drought.

Chapter Two
Yesterday's Warning Signs

OUTER BANKS OF NORTH CAROLINA, 1590— The *Moonlight*, a resupply ship, swung to her anchors three leagues off a dark continent. From its deck John White looked ashore and saw a plume of smoke rising from Roanoke Island, "neere the place where I left our Colony." (White spelled words in the sixteenth century manner, under English rules that have changed since his time.) He grew restless. White yearned to discover the fate of those he had been forced to abandon three years earlier. The eighty-nine men, seventeen women, and eleven children (including White's infant granddaughter) constituted America's first real settlement, backed by Queen Elizabeth, in a bold attempt to gain power in the New World. They had all arrived with guns,

John White returned to Roanoke Island in 1590 to rejoin the men and women he had left three years earlier. But no trace was ever found of the colonists.

steel, and immunity to the germs that would wipe out much
of America's indigenous population, but these first British
colonists had been woefully unprepared for the unnatural combination of forces that would swiftly obliterate them from the
face of the earth.

Having read reports of previous scouting voyages, White's
pioneers had set sail for the New World in 1587 with visions
of landing in an "Earth's only paradise," where "the earth
bringeth forth all things in abundance as in the first creation,
without toil or labour." The "luscious" humid land smelled
"like some delicate garden" full of fragrant flowers and grapes.
A great supply of fish and game beckoned. Even natives White
had earlier befriended, such as one Manteo, appeared "most
gentle, loving, and faithful, void of all guile and treason and
such as lived after the manner of the Golden Age." Europe had
at last discovered its biblical Eden.

Yet upon landing, White's settlers had found turmoil.
Bleached bones lay scattered near the scouts' decaying fort.
Deer grazed wrinkled melons that had grown up through the
floors of abandoned huts. The once babbling brooks had dwin-
dled to silence. Nowhere was the grassy "greene soil on the
hils" that once yielded abundant game. Visions of Eden, "the
most plentiful, sweet, wholesome and fruitful of all the world,"
had shriveled up. Undaunted, White had brought everyone
ashore to camp to make the best of a desolate situation. His
men had built crude structures. They had ploughed the dry
soil. But as weeks passed, the situation rapidly deteriorated.
His Roanoke Colony had arrived too late to plant crops. The
Caribbean's hostile Spanish garrisons had refused to sell salt,
cattle, plants, and water casks. Facing thirst, hunger, and
depleted water supplies, the settlers sent White for help.

Back in London his resupply mission got hijacked by history. Queen Elizabeth commandeered his ship to defend
England against the Spanish Armada. While White tried in
vain to hire boats to rescue Roanoke settlers abandoned on
this side of the Atlantic, his three-month journey dragged into

an agonizing three years. Finally he crossed, saw the smoke plume and, after years assuming the worst, his spirits leapt. He could hardly sleep, bursting with "good hope that some of the Colony were there expecting my returne out of England."

The next morning at dawn White and two captains set out to explore the island. They fired signal shots to announce their arrival. No response. The men rowed against a frustrating undertow. Halfway across, White noticed a second plume from a nearby chain of sand dunes and, thinking it a smoke signal, aimed for it. Getting nowhere by sea, they pulled ashore and walked the distance on foot, growing exhausted and thirsty in the midsummer heat. The fire "was much further . . . then we supposed it to be, so that we were very sore tired before wee came to the smoke. But that which grieved us more was that when we came to the smoke, we found no man nor signe that any had bene there lately, nor yet any fresh water in all this way to drinke."

In his three-year absence Roanoke had gone dry. The so-called Earthly Paradise had become a parched, depopulated, and ash-filled mausoleum. The place was so dry that over the next few days White's journal filled with descriptions of sailors wasting precious hours obsessed not with rescuing survivors but of desperately securing supplies of fresh water. There was a frenzy to the task: finding water; carefully storing water in casks; seeking out new sources of fresh water; rationing water; braving storm-tossed seas between ship and land, sacrificing several lives, just to retrieve more casks of fresh water.

Finally, on the morning of what might have been his granddaughter's third birthday, White navigated shoreboats to the Roanoke Island site. They found no life amidst the dry and deserted ruins, but Smith urged the crew to instead scour the barks of trees for a "secret token." Before his hasty departure White's colony agreed to carve the destination where they could be found, and one of his sailors noticed a tree that

This romanticized illustration shows an empty, abandoned fort that John White discovered when he returned to Roanoke Island. The only clue to the disappearance of the colonists was the word "CROATOAN" carved on a tree.

"had the barke taken off, and 5 foote from the ground in fayre Capitall letters was graven CROATOAN."

White was thrilled; his thirst-wracked Colonists had fallen upon the mercy of his friend Manteo's indigenous tribe, and he urged the sailors to head immediately fifty miles inland. He felt desperate to complete the search, rescue, resupply, and reestablishment of the Colony and family as soon as possible. But weather dictated otherwise. A massive and violent wind-storm brewed, snapping cables, breaking anchors, and, once again, sacrificing the ship's already depleted drinking supply.

"The weather grew to be fouler and fouler; our victuals scarse, and our caske and fresh water lost: it was therefore determined that we should goe for Saint John or some other land to the Southward for fresh water."

Upon refilling their water casks in the Azores, *Moonlight* caught the autumn trade winds to Europe. White never returned. He died in Ireland, dejected and defeated, survived only by his writings. His last enduring document was a long letter, filled with descriptive passages and illustrations describing the circumstances around his frustrated and futile efforts to help America's first colony survive its partial birth, cut short by conditions beyond their control.

Consider White's last impressions as he sailed away from the end of his bloodline and the failure of America's first colony: wracked by thirst; politically overruled by a parched and mutinous crew; facing limited supplies of fresh water; leaving behind a scorched arid landscape; astounded at how such a lush, fertile, and well-watered landscape could turn so hot, so dry, so desiccated, so fast; and wondering what powerful and deadly forces could have scattered Eden to the winds.

(continued on page 28)

Tracking a Global Extinction Force

Roanoke had precedents. Long before any Europeans set foot on the continent, various native settlements had grown to prominence only then to go swiftly extinct. Something in the Southwest made the great Anasazi and the Hohokam civilizations suddenly disperse, leaving behind empty ruins like a discarded shell, with no written records to reveal what ultimately sealed their fate.

What's more, America was only one part of a larger phenomenon. In the thirteenth century of what is present-day Cambodia, the once mighty and complex city of Angkor had gone into rapid and permanent decline until today only their impressive stone temples remain. Askun, the first African state in what is now Ethiopia, rose to grandeur over centuries, trading luxury goods with Rome and Persia, but in AD 750 it, too, went into decline and collapsed five decades later. A similar fate met the glorious reign in southern Africa of Great Zimbabwe and the regional capital Mapungubwe near the Limpopo River. So it went with ancient cities surrounding the Mediterranean and the Indus Valley: civilizations swelled to greatness, and then vanished without a trace.

Historians long assumed warfare was to blame, but paleo-climatologists–scientists who study the climate of past ages–discovered a pattern emerging. Askum declined in direct proportion to the drop in precipitation; as rain refused to fall, the city collapsed. Similar data has recently found that Angkor's mysterious end came not due to invasion by rival Siamese and Champa kingdoms, as long suspected, but from the fact that its canals and reservoirs ran dry. The same arid conditions shattered societies from Mapungubwe and Great Zimbabwe in Africa to the Anasazi and Hohokam in America.

Looking back through time, researchers have found that one recurring natural event has shaped human species more decisively and fundamentally than otherwise more dramatic disasters like fires or floods, volcanoes or earthquakes, receding glaciers or rising sea levels, relentless heat waves and unremitting cold snaps. The deadliest and most destructive force was the combination of heat and drought that led to water depletion. It is believed drought is what drove the first humans out of trees, then out of Africa, and finally out of any settlement that relied too recklessly and too precariously on water. ∎

America was haunted by the fate of Roanoke. Many assumed White's colonists had drowned, or had been killed by the Spanish, by hurricanes, or by hostile natives and lay buried in unmarked graves. Some clung to White's hope that the colonists had dispersed inland, merging with local Indian tribes who had learned to endure the New World's hard times.

For four centuries historians and archaeologists scoured the archives of time. Like forensic detectives, they pieced together bits and fragments: sixteenth-century copper coins, rings and tools; maps, title deeds, letters, rusty armor, bones; oral narratives, sketches, music, and linguistics. One provocative clue surfaced from what was believed to be a sixteenth-century well–submerged in the shallows just offshore due to erosion or poor planning–which suggested Roanoke's freshwater supply turned undrinkable before its time. But all these external clues lacked coherence, and could be dismissed as "speculative." Some gave up the search. It seemed as time went by that no one would ever really know what went awry for The Lost Colony.

But David Stahle, a University of Arkansas professor who specializes in the analysis of tree-ring records to determine past weather patterns, had other ideas. Rather than dig down into the earth for clues about Roanoke's fate, he believed the answers might emerge—just as John White had advised—through "secret tokens" embedded in the trees. But instead of Roman letters or a Maltese cross, he planned to carve out a cross-section of the tree trunk itself. Stahle was armed with new technology and belonged to a new breed of scientific researchers, paleoclimatologists, who cut slices into the earth and painstakingly collected and assembled them. Paleoclimatologists interpreted these clues— ice cores, sediment layers, pollen, lake beds, ocean floors and cylinders or wedges from trees—and then deciphered the cryptic hieroglyphics of, say, tree rings to translate the stories inscribed within. By cross-referencing hard data from samples, they could reconstruct the natural stage on which humans acted and evolved.

Stahle's team compared past and present conditions. Thumbing through tree ring pages of pre-history, they correlated thick and thin tree rings with unprecedented certainty about temperature, precipitation, and climate over the last eight centuries. An accurate detailed weather report emerged, month by month, starting three hundred years before Columbus set sail up to the present, and revealed the desperate situation both when White left Roanoke and when he returned three years later.

White had last seen his colonists on August 22, 1587, the end of a summer that data revealed as "the most extreme growing-season drought in 800 years," and during his three-year absence the drought had worsened. It killed vegetation, helped dry lightening ignite what White mistook for signal fires, and made sailors struggle to find "water to drinke." It explained why relations among natives had grown tense. And it showed how florid descriptions of the New World Eden became obsolete overnight.

White's chosen location and timing, wrote Stahle, could not possibly have been worse; fierce hot aridity beat down across North America, but grew worse at Roanoke. From 1185 to 1984 the Colonists precariously arrived in, and were abandoned during, that region's driest three-year episode of the last eight centuries. America's first colony possessed the technology to fend off human foes, but hunger and thirst pulled it apart in the face of humankind's deadliest enemy: water depletion. Those who settled new lands often went there seeking valuable resources, but neglected one that seemed so common as to be taken for granted.

Two centuries after Roanoke, one of history's greatest economists wrote about humanity's blind spot long after the failure of the Lost Colony. Adam Smith was at his desk in his study, stumped. The father of economics, whose classic *The Wealth of Nations* still dominates modern thinking, could not figure out why a diamond, "which has scarce any value in use," was worth more than water, of which "nothing is more useful." He called this absence of logic the paradox of value.

Other paradoxes of water involved: how an element so everpresent could become so scarce; how a resource so renewable can yet be finite; and how something so precious can remain, for so many, so priceless.

(continued on page 36)

Engineered Solutions and Technological Wonders

America came to rely on a primary arsenal of formidable hard infrastructure weapons that could be called the five Ds—dikes, diversions, deep-well drills, desalination (salt removal), and above all: dams. All these technologies had been known for millennia. Diversions predated Roman aqueducts; wells were prehistoric; Archimedes' ancient Egyptian screw lifted water from rivers and wells into furrows; sailors could capture and drink the water vapor boiled from a kettle dipped in the sea; and water storage dams in Jordan, Egypt, and other parts of the Middle East date back 5,000 years.

But industrial age America ratcheted up each undertaking into a kind of arms race against Mother Nature that continues to this day. Today, almost every river in the U.S. has been plugged, diked, diverted, or dewatered by anywhere from 78,000 to 2.5 million dams. The resulting fragmentation water depletion means major rivers like the Colorado or Rio Grande no longer reach the sea, and aquatic freshwater species are the most endangered on earth.

Worldwide the story is similar. Libya, in north Africa, pumped water from beneath the Sahara into the Great Man-Made River. Johannesburg diverted sources of the Orange River from the Atlantic to the Indian Oceans. From Sydney to Beijing, Mexico City to New Delhi, global leaders embraced infrastructure technology as "modern temples" and "20th century pyramids."

Collectively, all nations gave rise to 49,000 dams larger than a four-story building, depleting freshwater seas while concentrating and altering the flow of rivers to the point where, scientists confirm, the weight of this water infrastructure has displaced 80 million people, triggered man-made earthquakes, and perhaps even altered the very orbit of the Earth. ■

Large blocks of Welsh slate were used to construct the Dam at Lake Vyrnwy in North Wales, in the United Kingdom. Built between 1881 and 1888, it was the first large stone-built dam in the U.K.

As the United States grew, expanded west, and developed economically, a unifying goal of its urban society became the overarching priority to tap our ingenuity, insulate cities from aridity, and escape the potential depletion of water. Put simply, America's city, state, and federal governments declared war on drought.

New agencies were endowed with vast funds and authority to deploy cutting-edge tools to find and secure water. No obstacle was too big. Government workers drained swamps. They turned deserts into oases. They diverted one river into a second. They defied gravity. In some cases they reversed the flow of rivers. In others they made water flow uphill and over mountains.

Some called this extraordinary political phenomenon the birth of the "hydraulic mission" or the era of "heroic engineering." It grew most rapidly at the start of the twentieth century in the arid American West, and at the heart of the largest desert civilization, in Los Angeles.

At the end of the Civil War, Los Angeles was best described as a sleepy and filthy little pueblo of 13,000 people. Two decades later the railroad connected it to the rest of the country, a real estate boom was followed by an oil boom, and the only thing holding it back from another explosive boom was the geographic reality of it being surrounded on three sides by desert and on its other side by the Pacific Ocean. The nearest big and reliable source of fresh water, the Owens River, lay a staggering 250 miles away.

Into that arid world came William Mulholland, a charismatic but initially unfocused drifter who worked on a crew drilling deep wells and began his career at a private water company digging ditches and clearing debris from canals. From up close, Mulholland saw how water moved, and how man's moving of water transformed impoverished land, and people, into a rich and powerful force. He was not wasteful, and in fact was an early water conservation advocate who preferred recharging aquifers to storing water in dams that could quickly fill with silt or evaporate.

The population of Los Angeles doubled to 200,000 between 1900 and 1904, and it threatened to collapse under dry, hot conditions and geographic misfortune. But Mulholland was "about to become a modern Moses. . . . instead of leading his people through the waters to the promised land, he would cleave the desert and lead the promised waters to them."

To pass a bond issue to build aqueducts, Mulholland's men sponsored and starred in their own short propaganda film. *Thirst* played in L.A.'s theaters between newsreels and feature movies. It warned that without the infusion of expensive, distant imported water, the city would dry up and blow away.

On November 5, 1913, the Los Angeles Department of Water and Power completed a 250-mile-long pipeline to secure California's future. The canal diverted the Owens River to the San Fernando Valley, in effect stealing other people's water. The villages along the Owens would dry up, freshwater trout fisheries would collapse, and the ecologically fragile Mono Lake would slowly vanish, sending dust storms into the sky with no end in sight.

Upon turning the valve on that historic day, Mulholland spread his arms and famously said to the people of Los Angeles, "There it is. Take it."

They took it: to grow crops and feed cattle; to build industrial movie studios; to pave roads and build houses, with showers and flush toilets; to sprinkle lawns and lush gardens beside swimming pools; to wash cars and to hose down their driveways.

Four months after diverting the Owens River, Mulholland was among the most powerful, and least humble, men in America, having unlocked the great city's future through innovation and iron will. Yet no sooner had Mulholland diverted one river than he came under pressure to secure even more water for the expanding, sprawling thirsty city.

The first Los Angeles
Acqueduct, designed by
William Mulholland,
cascades near Sylmar, in
the San Fernando Valley
region of Los Angeles.

In San Franciquito Canyon his St. Francis Dam was already under construction, but he decided to raise it higher and make it bigger until it would store more and more water, gathering three year's worth of scattered rainfall into 11.4 billion gallons of water that, in March of 1928, began to leak. Mulholland ignored the leak when his inspectors reported it until it could not be ignored, bursting through the dam in a surge of water two hundred feet high, engulfing the town, demolishing more than a thousand homes, and washing them all, along with 8,000 acres of topsoil, out to sea. Bodies would wash up on beaches days later.

Mulholland, the man who set out to conquer drought, had instead been profoundly humbled, broken by the will of water. The restless and fast growing city, like all American cities, woke up realizing the full extent of its vulnerability to increasingly scarce water, constant growth, ferocious thirst, and a warming, drying climate, under which it lingers to this day.

A 1926 colorized photo of St. Francis Dam, located forty miles northwest of Los Angeles near the city of Santa Clarita.

Water Rights and Water Wrongs

To understand how Los Angeles acquired the liquid treasure it would divert to itself, it's worth understanding a unique invention from the American West called the "water right."

This right is a legally recognized and defensible title to use a certain amount of water from a river flowing in an arid land. The rights grew out of conflict, when farmers, ranchers, and miners all fought to divert a finite supply of scarce water. To avert bloodshed, courts granted the property deeds, or water rights, based on the concept "first in time, first in right." The oldest users of the river held a seniority position, and this water was theirs so long as they used it productively.

Farmers in the sunny, fertile Owens Valley used their water productively, but Mulholland believed he could do far more with less. He didn't announce this in an open public debate, of course. Instead his men lied about their motives, practiced spying and deception, offered bribes, concealed their intent, quietly bought up all the lands with water rights attached to them, and prepared to divert the sleepy rural river into the teeming metropolis that was growing, fast, to 500,000 people.

People in Owens Valley gradually caught on to the tricks, but greed played neighbor against neighbor in who could sell off their land and water title rights for the highest price to those "foolish" men visiting from the city, and by the time anyone tried to put a stop to it, the deed was done. Even before the ink signatures were dry, teams of eighteen or more mules were being hitched to sections of the Los Angeles Aqueduct, to lug them into place. When these were assembled the stage was set. ■

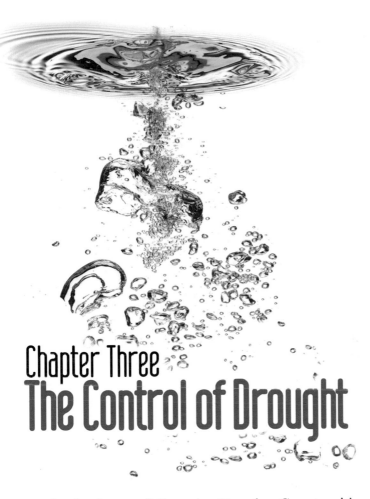

Chapter Three
The Control of Drought

In the heart of Georgia, Douglas County citizens felt uncomfortable at how government kept close watch over their water use. But political leaders told them to get used to it. Security depended on collective enforcement of rules, and everyone had to obey. Indeed, rather than resist, otherwise patriotic people chose instead to call up a hotline and turn in neighbors they suspected were breaking the law. Authorities had unleashed silent patrols to search up and down suburban streets, looking for offenders. When they caught one red-handed, creeping out in the middle of the night to turn on their lawn sprinkler, they closed in fast and . . . shut off the taps.

By November of 2007 water scarcity was no laughing matter for millions in the southeastern United States. Water pressure throughout the normally lush subcontinent was growing anemic, with three quarters of the region considered "drought affected" and a fourth in the most extreme category: "exceptional" drought. The lack of water wrought serious consequences both for the booming economy and its civic cohesion. Seventeen North Carolina water systems had less than three months left of water before they reached the dregs. Farmers began carting water around in barrels on the back of trucks, to keep their livestock alive. Tennessee towns restricted tap water to three hours per day. But at the epicenter of the worst crippling regional drought in a century sat the fastest growing and most vulnerable city in the U.S.: Atlanta.

Residents living in the sprawling metropolitan area drew their water supply from a man-made reservoir backed up by a dam built in the 1950s. But that reservoir, Lake Lanier, was never meant to slake the unlimited thirst of 5 million people today, nor could it absorb another 2 million inhabitants expected in the next two decades. State and local government agencies did their part, announcing modest but symbolic gestures. Gwinnett County Parks and Recreation shut down outdoor drinking fountains. The University of Georgia's homecoming event set in place a tiered policy of "No Flushing." All that still wasn't enough to stop depletion.

Ironically, the city's motto had always been "Atlanta grows where water goes." But no one had really considered a time when the water might stop flowing, and like Los Angeles's Mulholland, the civic leaders of Atlanta didn't want people to feel a sense of limitations on their freedom. So everyone used as much as they pleased. In October, well into the drought, prominent philanthropist Chris Carlos's 14,000-square-foot property sucked 440,000 gallons of water during that one month, 14,700 per day; journalists calculated that was enough to fill fifty-eight swimming pools. Publicly shamed, he vowed to mend his thirsty ways. "I honestly didn't realize the extent of my water use," said Carlos, "and regret I didn't act sooner."

Residences, parks, and schools were one thing. But most commercial enterprises could not exist without water, and went out of business, while survivors sought to showcase how austere they could be. Southeastern drought killed jobs throughout the region. As businesses wilted in Atlanta, multinationals like UPS Inc. installed waterless urinals, and saved 10,000 gallons a day by dry-mopping. The vast Stone Mountain Park canceled plans to manufacture a 1.2-million gallon mountain of snow. Landscapers fired 14,000 workers, and the earth's largest aquarium drained some of its new exhibits.

(continued on page 48)

Coke's Most Controversial Ingredient

Though its secret recipe remains locked in a vault, Coke's main ingredient is obvious to all. It requires twelve gallons of water to produce each sixteen ounce can or bottle, and the $23-billion company's four hundred beverage brands use more than 280 billion liters of water every year.

In the end, each Coke contains more than 70 percent fresh water. As it happens, each human contains roughly the same amount. Yet while Georgia's governor declared a state of emergency in eighty-five counties, urged people to forgo showers, car washes, lawns, and gardens, and prepared to ration household water, a few people questioned why Coke kept its bottling plant chugging along at full strength while individual people had to do more with less.

Global consumer agitation had created the same controversy for the company in Kerala, India, where a plant pumping water for bottling as Coke was charged with depriving surrounding communities of clean water. The company was also feeling the heat from protesters for filtering public taps into Desani Water—sold at four times the price of gasoline in the controversial $11-billion bottled-water industry.

Coca-Cola rushed to defray criticism, both in the U.S. and overseas. Then CEO Neville Isdell announced a $20 million partnership with the World Wildlife Fund to reduce 5 percent use for 18 percent efficiency, recycle wastewater at 85 percent of operations, and replenish seven critically key stressed watersheds in forty countries. Coke's foremost corporate identity campaign was "Make Every Drop Count."

Yet as Coke had to face this drought in its own backyard, it felt the limits to the company's austerity: it could do nothing about all the water used to grow the sugar cane it used to caramelize and sweeten its water. The private company's dependence on public goodwill and natural resources was absolute. At some point, without secure access to abundant clean freshwater, Coke would simply dry up. ■

But no global business was more financially, economically, and politically vulnerable to drought than the Atlanta-based global headquarters of the Coca-Cola Company.

The biggest threat to drought in the region was less economic than political. Atlanta urbanites blamed farmers, who blamed industry. The city elbowed surrounding counties. Georgia fought over water that flowed in rivers shared with Alabama and Florida and Tennessee.

The political effect of drought was unique among disasters. Terrorist attacks, hurricanes, earthquakes, or wildfires brought out the best in Americans; they pulled communities together and made the nation unite. By contrast, water depletion split people apart.

This was especially so when drought was largely a consequence of growth. Water scarcity was the result not simply of weather or food, but of too many people using too much water for too many diverse economic activities. The city, and the state, could no longer keep up with demand, but nor was it willing or able to rein in thirst. Soon the city was faced with sixty days left in Lake Lanier reservoir. Without the ability to ensure a reliable and abundant supply of water, the nation's fastest-growing city began coming apart at the seams. "We're taking hundreds of calls from people who are ratting out their neighbors," said Janet Ward, spokesperson for the Atlanta Department of Watershed Management. "People are angry. What do you expect? If your lawn is brown and blowing away, and the neighbor's is all green, you know what's going on."

As the city and state cried out for leadership, all eyes turned toward the governor's mansion. But Georgia's chief executive Sonny Perdue had ordered utilities to reduce water consumption by 10 percent across the board, or face fines—fines that were in turn shouldered by the population through those nighttime patrols. He had already declared a state of emergency for eighty-five counties, which didn't help. As these measures failed, the Baptist governor did what any

leader might do when confronting forces beyond his control. He gathered a large group of followers on the capitol steps, had everyone bow their head in prayer, and encouraged the city to seek help, begging a higher power to forgive the state its wasteful ways with water.

"We've come together here simply for one reason and one reason only," he said, "to very reverently and respectfully pray up a storm."

Farmers in some states don't crack down on consumption, scan the sky for clouds, or bow their heads to pray for rain. For decades the steady source of water that has irrigated their crops has come gushing forth from beneath their feet.

That invisible source, known commonly as groundwater, provides 95 percent of America's fresh water. Protected from evaporation by the sun, or transpiration by plants, the advantage of groundwater was that it stayed put. It stayed locked up below, filling a billion tiny packets in between unsorted clay, silt, sand, and gravel. Or it did right up until a city or farmer turned on the pumps that lifted groundwater to the surface.

That groundwater, unlike rain or snow, was emphatically reliable. It flowed twenty-four hours a day, seven days a week, 365 days a year. You could count on it to be there, which after 90,000 years of dependence on the whims of weather, felt miraculous.

Groundwater also has proven intensively productive. In the middle of a drought, High Plains farmers in eight midwestern states can still tap into one of the world's largest groundwater sources—the eight-hundred-mile-long Ogallala Aquifer—to irrigate their fields, and support a fifth of the wheat, corn, cotton, and cattle produced in the United States. Compared with rainwater farms, irrigated agriculture produced twice the amount of food on the same amount of land. In essence, Ogallala turned 14 million acres of farmland in the Midwest into the leading irrigation area in the western hemisphere, adding $20 million worth of food and fiber to the world's markets.

What is Groundwater?

People share misconceptions about aquifers, geological formations that hold groundwater. Some picture a freshwater pond in a cavernous hollow hole; others imagine raging subterranean rivers; still more consider groundwater and surface water to be totally unrelated.

In reality, rivers and groundwater are intimately connected, and feed one another. The best way to understand groundwater is to dig in the sand beside a lake, river, or ocean. Whether fine sand or rocky pebbles, it gets damper the deeper you go. Water saturates and seeps down through the porous surface of the earth until it dries up, or gets stopped or deflected by an impermeable layer.

Once it sinks deep enough beneath the surface, groundwater may be protected from the hot sun, human pollution, and the deep roots of thirsty living plants and trees. It may be of an exceptional quality, but it also might be old.

Scientists try to determine water's approximate age, through isotopes, in order to gauge how much can be pumped. If ancient groundwater is pumped down and out faster than it can be renewed and replenished by younger generations, sustainable pumping degrades to water mining. ■

There was just one catch. Irrigated productivity also used three times the amount of water as rain-fed farms. That water was borrowed from an earlier age. Scientists say the Ogallala Aquifer took 6,000 years to fill. Geologists have found that the water is geologic, or fossil water, and thus limited.

Today the only nagging issue these breadbasket farmers confront as they cultivate the earth and feed the world is how long the miracle will last before their water runs out. Fearing the answer, some no longer ask.

Big as it was, the Ogallala Aquifer was limited. It filled up between 10 and 3 million years ago, from streams that no longer flow. So while moderate rain and snowfall might still sink a few inches into the damp surface, the deeper aquifer is no longer being recharged.

Meanwhile, ever since the 1940s, it has been depleted and polluted at an astonishing rate. All the pesticides and surface pollution trickles down, posing a threat to the municipal users who rely on groundwater for drinking. More importantly, farmers extract 12 billion cubic meters—the equivalent of eighteen Colorado Rivers—each year for their irrigation. In parts of Kansas, New Mexico, Oklahoma, and Texas the aquifer has plunged more than one hundred feet. It continues to sink throughout the region at an average of 2.7 feet per year. Already 9 percent of the Aquifer has been burned up forever, and the demand for its productivity only escalates with global hunger. Today some 200,000 wells are pumping around the clock, and some estimate that within twenty-five years the aquifer will be dry.

As the aquifer continues to vanish, several things happen. Wells grow less and less reliable. Because aquifers are connected to surface water in lower elevations, stream flows decline. When the water is removed from the pockets beneath the surface, there is nothing to hold up all the weight above, leading to compaction and ground subsidence. Without the dilution of large amounts of water, pollution concentrates and leads to water-quality deterioration of supplies that provide

drinking water for 82 percent of the population.

On the surface, costs go up for farmers and cities as they are forced to lift and purify the water. We often forget it, but water is incredibly heavy: three hundred gallons weighs a ton. So to lift the same amount of water each day from deeper and deeper levels requires more and more energy. Wells on thousands of farms and towns have gone dry. Local farmers file for bankruptcy and property values plummet. Economies are stifled. One part of Texas planned a nuclear plant with hopes that it could sell energy to the rest of the U.S. The city had taken care of all safety measures, but hadn't fully taken into account the impact of the water taking away what was available for municipal, agriculture, or industry.

With 95 percent of all economic activity depending on a fossil aquifer, planners can hardly stop pumping, especially if doing so cuts food supply even as hunger increases. So instead governments just try to delay the inevitable by encouraging efficiency and conservation: terracing, crop rotation, center pivot and drip irrigation, all of which have helped to slow aquifer depletion to a few feet lower each year.

(continued on page 58)

Exporting Virtual Water Embedded in Food

As farming converts more than 70 percent of all water into food, the result of the transformation is "virtual water." That term measures the amount of water embedded in the production of agricultural products. It adds up daily, and is useful.

Consider the amount of virtual water embedded in just one healthy American breakfast. A bowl of Rice Krispies with milk (grown with 350 gallons of virtual water). Dry grounds for a cup of coffee (37 gallons). Eggs and toast and a side of bacon (470 gallons). Then there's lunch, say, a quick stop at McDonald's, where a Big Mac requires 2,600 gallons of virtual water.

Worldwide, a healthy diet of 3,000 calories requires roughly 1,000 gallons of virtual water; a vegetarian diet impacts the least, while a meat-based diet rich in corn-fed beef can require 4,000 gallons of water per person per day. Americans "eat" seventy times more water as food than we use to bathe and wash or drink. Now multiply that impact by 300 million Americans, 365 days a year.

Virtual water helps explain how 8 million New Yorkers or Los Angelinos deplete midwestern water supplies 1,000 miles away. As cities import and consume corn-fed beef or flour for bagels, they essentially eat some Ogallala Aquifer along with it.

Virtual water also links affluent appetites with Third World famine. When a 1,000-year-drought hit Australia, farmers were devastated and global wheat prices rose, affecting the price of bread in supermarkets worldwide. Due to China's groundwater depletion, which supports four-fifths of its irrigated land, that country lost the ability to feed itself; so it bought grain from elsewhere in the world, driving up the price of rice higher than many poor rural people in Africa or Asia could afford, leading to hunger and riots. ■

Many groundwater-dependent farmers fear for the fate of their children and grandchildren who will inherit their farms, and their irrigation pumps, even as the wells run dry. They know their aquifer can not last forever. They know the end is coming. They just don't know when.

Until then, they have no incentive to stop or even slow the gush of water lifted from beneath their feet and spread out on the land, where it evaporates, is converted into food, and, after harvest, is shipped off elsewhere in the world, never to return again.

Before becoming the first Nobel Prize winner to oversee the United States Department of Energy, Dr. Steven Chu directed the Lawrence Berkeley National Laboratory, arguably the Federal government's most pre-eminent research facility. He was a physicist by training. But he eventually grew far less concerned about understanding such astrophysical phenomena as black holes or quarks or (his specialty) how to cool and trap atoms with laser light. Those were important issues, but politically obscure. What bothered him was the uncertain fate of that rather mundane molecule—two parts hydrogen and one part oxygen—on which all life depends.

Chu lived and worked in the East Bay of San Francisco, which meant his existence depended on the local municipal water district. His supply of water accumulated and gathered in the cooler Sierra Nevada mountain range, the high altitude border between Nevada and California. Flows were never all that abundant in the semiarid state. What's more, the runoff still required treatment and artificial storage, since a staggering 90 percent of California's purifying, filtering, and sponge-like wetlands had disappeared under the onslaught of development and agriculture. But for much of the last century the supply had at least been somewhat reliable. As snow slowly melted each spring it was channeled into reservoirs and aqueducts and then pipes, into the homes, laboratories, and offices of 30 million people just like Chu.

(continued on page 64)

Dr. Steven Chu

Climate Change and Water Depletion

Since the dawn of the industrial age, humankind has been burning wood, coal, oil, and other fossil fuels at an unprecedented rate. The smoke and other pollution thicken the protective layer of the atmosphere in an effect that is like rolling up the car windows in a parking lot on a hot summer day. The result traps more heat than it releases. Hence: global warming.

Today most people grasp that greenhouse gas pollution causes global warming, and accept the need to cut future emissions. But few seem prepared to absorb or adapt to the hydrological impacts that will occur even if all pollution ended immediately.

Those consequences are both real and unavoidable. The year 2008 witnessed Indian farmland drying up, Australian wildfires, African flash floods, Asian disease vectors, Andean melting glaciers, Micronesian tidal surges, Indian coastal saline intrusion, and North American drought. Though wildly diverse in kind or place, these impacts all share one common denominator: water.

Initially, models suggested that a warmer world would lead to a wetter world. Perhaps globally it will be, as more rain falls on oceans, at the equator, and in polar extremes. But where most humans have settled, dryness has been worsening. Due primarily to heat, the amount of the Earth's land surface suffering drought has doubled in recent decades.

Worse, heat may thrust more water as vapor into the atmosphere, where it becomes another greenhouse gas. Unstable water is the unifying medium for climate change. Suddenly absent or overabundant water makes the abstract and invisible forces of climate change painfully clear. The coming extremes—whether escalating storms erode soils and overwhelm treatment plants or perpetual droughts dry up rivers and aquifers—cause the same undesirable outcome: resource scarcity.

The reality of global warming poses a quadruple threat to water scarcity. The danger of sudden storms prompts dam operators to keep reservoirs artificially low in order to absorb potential surges. In the wet months, the higher danger of extreme sudden storms makes dam operators lower dams to absorb potentially big flood surges. In the dry months, hotter temperatures dry up soil moisture, reduce runoff, and evaporate what little water was stored in the reservoir. The faster transpiration by plants, trees, and crops increases agricultural demand for supplementary water. And water scarcity speeds up the decline of biodiversity, so that the listing and protection of endangered species further reduces water supplies. We can store far less water even as we demand far more.

That is why when scientists like Chu advocate climate change prevention, they really mean slashing dirty energy consumption. When they worry about climate adaptation, they mean water depletion. ∎

Drought has claimed all but a few puddles
of water near Salar de Uyuni, in southwest
Bolivia, near the crest of the Andes.

No longer. In recent years scientists have been document-ing how the all critical "snowpack" was being defrosted. The decline of winter's frozen white powder in the Sierra and Rocky Mountains undermined a kind of "natural infrastruc-ture" or "water towers" that supplied the American West. By May 2007, Chu noted with increasing concern how the Sierra snowpack had fallen lower than at any time in the last twenty years. Warmer temperatures, combined with increas-ing accumulations of dark dust, meant that snow came later, melted sooner, and was hastened off by rain.

Climate change modeling was an inexact science, but even the most conservative readings suggested that warm-ing conditions would only worsen as the century continued. Over the next seven decades, some 30 to 70 percent of the snowpack would disappear. "There's a two-thirds chance there will be a disaster," Chu told a *New York Times* reporter, "and that's in the best scenario."

Chu and thousands of other reputable scientists have grown certain in the last few decades that one driving force lay behind the incrementally rising heat, the delayed winters, the premature springs, the conversion of snow and ice into rain, and the longer summers: climate change.

The most popularized fear has been rising sea levels—the result both of melting polar ice caps and the expansion of warmer oceans. This gradual phenomenon poses grave dan-ger to coastal cities from Miami and New York to Seattle and San Francisco Bay. It may threaten low-lying islands and countries like Bangladesh and the Netherlands. Those populations may migrate inland, but saltwater would still infiltrate groundwater and delta estuaries on which millions of even high-elevation people depend. Also, plants and ani-mals that we depend on would become vulnerable, causing ripple effects up the economic supply chain. Trees and grain undergo sudden growth spurts from the larger downpours, but their swollen biomass would become a tinderbox or wilt during the ensuing dry spells, leading respectively to forest fires or crop failures.

Less noticed, the hydrological cycle is accelerating into a state of extremes. With rising heat, more water evaporates faster into the sky. In soggy regions, that water then falls again harder and often more violently in wet seasons—leading to increasingly less manageable floods and hurricanes like that which paraylzed New Orleans. In arid regions less

When Hydropower Emits Greenhouse Gas

The connection between water and energy calls to mind the image of a hydroelectric power dam. Hydropower's supporters describe it as a clean alternative to burning fossil fuels like dirty coal, gas, or oil. Indeed, turbines can tap renewable energy of rivers in a way that reduces the risk of climate change. But the transaction is rarely simple.

For starters, fewer than 2 percent of U.S. dams produce any power at all. Some that do, in California, use more energy to transport water than they generate.

Also, while some dispute the findings, all existing peer-reviewed scientific research has demonstrated how warm, shallow, stagnant reservoirs behind some large dams can flood such vast areas of vegetation that they generate methane, an extremely potent greenhouse gas twenty-three times more potent than carbon, with impacts worse than some traditional oil or coal-burning thermal plants.

Finally, hydropower becomes vulnerable to fluctuating rivers; when water runoff is depleted to a weak trickle that can't turn turbines, entire areas are plunged into darkness.

As secretary of energy, Chu was caught in the middle of this complex global debate. To help humankind adapt to water, he would have to recommend policies that would reform our approach to energy, and vice-versa. ■

water is less likely to fall anywhere at all, leading to protracted, perpetual, and permanent droughts.

To ensure 40 million Westerners have enough to drink, garden, bathe, or use in an office, water managers would like to capture and store more water behind newer and higher dams. Unfortunately they can't. The basis for plans has gone haywire, the best sites are already dammed, new construction costs too much, and they'd have to release water in anticipation of a sudden deluge. Infrastructure built to absorb a five-hundred-year-flood or store through a five-year drought now faces 2,000-year floods that the dams can't handle, followed by ten- or twenty-year droughts that cities can't withstand.

The obvious pollution risk of fossil fuels and the climate vulnerability of hydropower has led some politicians to embrace and subsidize what they consider "climate-friendly" energy solutions like biofuels, geothermal plants, wind, and solar. Yet betting on any one of these can have a heavy impact on water supplies.

Right now, biofuels, in particular corn-based ethanol, consume 2 percent of all irrigated water. Once that reserve is gone, it cannot be used for, say, drinking or growing vegetables or grains to eat. Worse, the United States and other nations have proposed plans to quadruple the amount of biofuels. In Chu's home of water-stressed California, proposed subsidies would lead the state to destroy 3 trillion gallons of water each year just to irrigate and produce so-called "clean" biofuels.

Beyond its other drawbacks—potential meltdown, safety hazards, and disposal of waste—nuclear power uses large amounts of water. A nuclear plant that generates 2,500 megawatts will consume 10 billion gallons of water per year, and because that water is finite, it will not be replenished. Even "greener" sources, like large geothermal and solar plants, prove to have devastating thirsts. One California solar energy plant consumes 90,000 gallons per megawatt per year simply to rinse its reflective mirrors. Billions more gallons are required to cool the power-generating plants in the middle of the desert. Geothermal plants use the naturally high temperatures emanating from the magma-filled core of the earth to heat water into steam, and use that pressure to turn turbines. But these large plants also run out of water during the summer, demanding billions of gallons piped from lakes, streams, and aquifers to generate the steam.

Even before Chu was sworn into office as secretary of energy in January 2009, there was no question that the energy and water challenges were inextricably woven together. A fifth of all energy in California is devoted to moving, lifting, heating, and treating water; meanwhile, two-fifths of all water in the state is used to cool plants or turn turbines. Any effort to reverse water or energy depletion would somehow need to combine the two. The secret perhaps lies in setting up more efficient ways that encourage consumers and producers to use less of each. By cutting either water or energy demand in half, for example, Americans also would simultaneously cut energy consumption by a tenth and water use by a fifth, respectively. Changing behavior might not be easy, but it would be far less painful and frightening than the alternatives.

Chapter Four
Tomorrow's Potential Outcomes

In 1983, a sudden unmanageable flood nearly caused the collapse of Glen Canyon Dam on the Colorado River. Had the dam failed, it would have resulted in a hydraulic "domino effect," as a wall of water hundreds of feet high would have crashed through the Grand Canyon until it encountered Lake Mead and then went on to obliterate Hoover Dam as well, leaving millions of people high and dry. Such collapses are far from unusual. All dams die, some spectacularly, although old age means their end usually arrives on a smaller scale, under a gradual timetable and in less dramatic fashion.

Dams as Ticking Time Bombs

The Bureau of Reclamation estimates 2,000 dams have collapsed since the Middle Ages, with two hundred large dam failures in the first eight decades of the last century. The spectacular failures of St. Francis Dam in Southern California, and of Teton Dam in Idaho each led to safety measures that have alleviated the risk in America to some extent, but the dangers continue to grow in proportion to the scale of the dam and the number of people who continue to move into the rich floodplain downstream, assuming they are on safe ground. This could be a mistake.

Dams fail for a variety of reasons. Time adds wear and tear; sediment piles upstream; both are exacerbated by climate change. In three decades, 85 percent of all U.S. dams will have outlived what engineers consider to be their average fifty-year lifespan. The American Society of Civil Engineers recently graded dams with a D because they put lives, property, and the natural environment at risk. ■

Glen Canyon Dam, on the
Colorado River, Arizona

The Glen Canyon Dam rises 710 feet high to block the flow of the Colorado River. It is the fourth-highest dam in the U.S.

When vast quantities of stored water suddenly vanish, cities face the natural condition of aridity. The more dependent society becomes on an artificial civil works project, the more exposed it is when that centralized water infrastructure fails. The one certainty of extreme climate change is its extreme uncertainty. Summers will get hotter, droughts will last longer, and floods will grow more intense. To absorb unpredictable deluges, responsible dam operators have been forced in anticipation to lower their storage capacity and release waters in the spring—exactly the time when people depend on reservoirs the most.

Some reputable hydrologists try to predict what happens if—some say *when*—Folsom Dam gives way and Sacramento is inundated. Others project how rising sea levels infiltrate the freshwater pumps and groundwater aquifers of coastal cities in America's fastest-growing states of California, Texas, and Florida. By 2017 or 2021, others anticipate how, under the rising heat of climate change, mega-dams like Hoover and Glen Canyon will fill up with sediment and evaporate beyond a point of no return, too low to spill water or turn hydropower turbines and not high enough to reach the intake pipes that carry water to cities like Las Vegas. Writers who anticipate the consequences of dams' demise describe such "Dead Pools" or "Great Thirsts" leading to pivotal, sudden transformations.

Despite the exorbitant costs, the escalating thirst for more water typically has renewed political interest in infrastructure. For civil engineers, anything remains possible. Some advocate tens of thousands of new smaller dams to capture sediment before it can eat into reservoir storage capacity. Others attempt to invent a giant Saran Wrap to prevent water from boiling away under the sun. And not only must the world erect 45,000 more dams, it must unlock funds for large-scale water transfers that divert one river into another.

Pipe Dreams for Re-plumbing the World

One method communities use to meet water demand is to divert water from one river basin to another. This is called an interbasin water transfer, and the transfer often occurs where communities are located on a ridgeline between two river basins.

Transfer of water from one basin to another is not a new phenomenon. After World War II, California shunted water from the raging Trinity River into the Sacramento River. In the early 1960s, North American Water and Power Alliance drew up plans to dam and divert the Yukon River from eastern Alaska to be sent down giant canals and aqueducts to water the American Southwest. Later the Great Recycling and Northern Development (GRAND) Canal proposed backing up Lake Superior out into the western prairies of Canada and the United States.

The latter two large-scale visions collapsed under the sheer weight of the volume of water they wanted to move, and under the burden of their massive $400 billion price tags. But they succeeded in searing in the mindset that rivers that reached the sea were "wasted" and that water that wasn't tapped was "surplus." California is again trying to raise another $6 billion to raise dam walls, pour new concrete infrastructure, and divert Northern California water in a Peripheral Canal to Los Angeles. ■

Dams and diversions are not the only technological supply-side approaches. And while most remain off-limits because they are impractical, or expensive, a large voting bloc during drought makes politicians reset the margins of what may be possible. A few supply schemes propose hauling giant icebergs south, then piping their freshwater runoff to the city's inhabitants (they're melting anyway, goes the thinking). Other entrepreneurs envision filling giant plastic bags and towing them. Cloud seeding continues to have its litigious and entrepreneurial supporters who take an increasingly scientific approach to the art of rainmaking.

Perhaps the most tantalizing option for boosting supply remains groundwater, the source of 95 percent of America's water. Some geologists claim that ten to twenty times the amount of surface water sits quietly, waiting unseen and unused, in the pores between rock and sand. But the apparent abundance may be deceptive. Any soluble chemical, biological, or mineral pollution can trickle through the earth, pulled down by gravity, to contaminate the freshwater; and once tainted, contaminated aquifers are notoriously hard to make pure again. The second challenge is water's age. Countless wells that sink down the equivalent of round-the-clock sucking straws can deplete a so-called fossil aquifer in a matter of months. And when it's gone, it's gone.

Desalination—removal of salt from seawater—entices modern civilizations as the ultimate temptation. First, there's the ocean, with the potential to supply more than we could ever use. Second, most of the population and economic growth seems to be gravitating toward the coasts, especially in the U.S. Third, it seems a small technological step and affordable price to pay to purify the ocean. And, as a bonus, there may even be a demand for the salt.

Yet again complications arise. The force required to separate salt from water is one kilowatt-hour to produce 250 gallons. Since energy plants burn fossil fuels, desalination increases greenhouse gas emissions in ways that further deplete natural water supply. Worse, the plants supplying the energy for desalination require additional freshwater infusions to operate. Thus, desalination reduces freshwater and generates pollution at the energy source in order to produce freshwater and aquatic waste somewhere else.

Desalination, the Elusive Mirage

There are today 12,300 desalination plants in 155 countries that combined produce 47 million cubic meters of water each day. A sixth of these plants ring Saudi Arabia, yielding a fourth of all desalinated water. California has thirty large-scale desalination plants in the planning stage. Demand is projected to grow 25 percent each year.

Yet taken as a whole, the desalination plants provide only 0.3 percent of the world's freshwater use. While astronomical costs are coming down rapidly, ranging from $0.50-1.00 per cubic meter, depending on the price of energy, the technology is still prohibitive to rich and poor nations alike, due largely to its economic and ecological impacts, respectively.

To slake an hour's thirst, a city the size of Sydney, Australia, will burn 255,000 tons of greenhouse gases. The byproduct of desalination is a kind of toxic chemical slurry, with chemicals and heavy metals that pose a threat to marine and terrestrial ecosystems. For every gallon of clean water, desalination pumps another gallon of this waste back into the surf.

"Desalination is not the answer to our water problems," writes John Archer in *Twenty-Thirst Century: The Future of Water in Australia*. "It is survival technology, a life support system, an admission of the extent of our failure." ∎

Pictured here is one of six desalination plants in operation in Dubai, which is located along the southern coast of the Persian Gulf.

Rather than working hard against nature, some supply-boosting techniques work with it. These soft approaches seek to mimic the natural pulse and turn seasonal rhythms to our advantage. Low dams capture rain and snowmelt from rivers, but quickly release this water in flows or artificial pumps to "recharge" nearby floodplains and groundwater tables. Those bodies of "natural infrastructure" preserve the integrity of the aquatic ecosystem, store water for human use, and yet do so while reducing the risk of sediment and cutting evaporation rates in half.

However, from new dams and towed icebergs to desalination plants and shared use of groundwater, new approaches may be needed. Societies may have to pass added regulations, recognizing that water is an economic resource. In short, halting depletion needs politics and price tags.

Chapter Five
Regulating Demand and Trading Water

Peter Brabeck-Letmathe, the chairman of Nestle, the multinational food supply conglomerate based in Switzerland, has warned the world's foremost corporate executives that the world faces dangerous limits to economic growth due to scarcity of just one resource: water.

Ironically, Nestle itself is seen as a real threat to unregulated economies, especially in U.S. regions previously not considered to be water scarce. For example, when Nestle decided to build bottled-water plants in rural Maine, Michigan, and Wisconsin, the idea was initially welcomed. In small towns the company would develop resources without causing obvious environmental damage. The process seemed clean: no pollution, no noise. And Nestle would create jobs worth $10-18 per hour in a time of stagnation. The company's plans were all based on taking water from a small well. But when executives announced plans to pump five hundred gallons per minute from that well, sixty minutes per hour, twenty-four hours per day, 365 days per year—more than a billion gallons every four years—people began to ask hard questions of each other, of the company, and of their government.

Environmentalists bemoaned the fate of their watershed as the groundwater table sank. Anglers grew concerned that their prize-winning trout streams would warm and wilt. What's more, people began to wonder if they were being cornered into accepting less than their fair share from the transaction. Nestle was one of three multinational bottled-water conglomerates in a global business generating huge profit margins on sales of $11 billion. As hydrologist Robert Glennon observed, "Bottled water has a higher retail value than milk, oil, gasoline, or, paradoxically, many commodities made with water, such as Coca-Cola."

But the root of the issue was about power and control. Nestle might risk turning the town into a kind of company store that charged its workers more for its products than they could earn in the factory. Even if they were paid $10 per hour by Nestle, the workers couldn't afford to buy water that retailed at $7.50 per gallon—especially since that pure, healthy spring water came from the ground beneath their homes. After all, the local water they would have to buy already belonged to them as a birthright. Or, at least they thought it did.

The law is seldom clear on this matter. The underlying question in Wisconsin, of "who owns the water," has become a national hot-button issue throughout the United States and the world. And few have a more absolute answer than Brabeck's counterpart across the ideological spectrum, Maude Barlow.

Barlow has become the de facto leader of a loose network of anti-globalization protesters, intellectuals, public utility employees, religious leaders, peasant farmers, social activists, trade unions, and human rights advocates called the Global Water Movement. As *the* essential element without which no living thing can exist, water must be regulated for the people, by the government, and against economic interests, Barlow has argued. Her manifesto demanded: "The Earth's fresh water belongs to the Earth and all species, and therefore must not be treated as a private commodity to be bought, sold, and traded for profit . . . the global fresh water supply is a shared legacy, a public trust, and a fundamental human right."

> **Bottled water has a higher retail value than milk, oil, gasoline, or, paradoxically, many commodities made with water, such as Coca-Cola.**

Robert Glennon

In her travels and publications, Barlow highlights campaigns for better public regulation and democratic governance of water, from Atlanta and New Orleans to Camden, New Jersey, and Stockton, California. Many autonomous groups refer to themselves as "Friends of Locally Owned Water," or FLOW.

Maude Barlow

Not all are successful, and many are outspent by companies seeking to secure their economic interests. In Lexington, Kentucky, the company American Water argued that "if the primary avenue of attack is legal, the principal line of defense, and the obvious point of counter attack, is political."

The political arena is where the battle continues to simmer. Lobbyists are pressing in from all sides of the U.S. Congress, at the World Bank, within the World Trade Organization, at the World Water Forum, and against the United Nations to advocate new legally binding language that had been left out in wetter eras. Governments must protect equal public access to rivers, lakes and aquifers; equal shares of public water to drink, wash and bathe; and the inalienable right to water. Pro-government liberals worry less about climate-driven permanent droughts or wasteful overconsumption. To them, water depletion results from private greed and exploitation by business interests. "Basically we see water as an issue of human rights versus corporate rights," said Barlow. Indeed, "water is the most important human-rights issue of them all."

If so, there are cracks in this human right. For starters, the human right to water lacks any legal or historical precedent whatsoever. The Declaration of Independence, Bill of Rights, U.S. Constitution, and Universal Declaration of Human Rights contain not a single phrase related to the individual protection of water. That means the elaborate legislative groundwork for the right must start from scratch.

Another problem is liability. If a well-meaning government bureaucrat fails to deliver water because of extreme climate flux, or lack of money, or his own sheer incompetence, he or she could be prosecuted as a violator of human rights. The U.S. State Department has fought the right to water on these grounds: "it raises a number of complicated issues regarding the nature of that right, how that right would be enforced, and which parties would bear responsibility for ensuring these rights are met."

A third concern is daily quantity and expense. The amount of water embodied in this right could range from ten gallons for survival to 5,000 gallons to live in comfort. A right to water would carry costs for storing, pumping, purifying, transporting, and treating. These must be accounted for somewhere. Many cities are so saddled with debt from their already subsidized water that they can't maintain or repair existing pipes and plants to meet demand. Indeed, public water expenses outstripped U.S. current spending by $500-$800 billion. Due in large part to leaky infrastructure, thirty-six states expect to suffer water shortages in the next decade. If the world's utilities were forced to provide free water to all residents, most would quickly go bankrupt, or break down, causing massive institutional and economic collapse.

Free water might encourage waste. Whether rich or poor, people who don't pay for a resource tend to overuse it inefficiently. "Free water" could help cause the very scarcity it sought to avoid.

Finally, Barlow's formal, inalienable human right to government-regulated water may create a new and total dependency on a single state monopoly. That double burden puts government utilities in the impossible position of having to ration the very right they are compelled to ensure. Even a well-intentioned centralized state entity cannot meet the dynamic needs of 300 million American customers. Against that, the alternative offered by market-like options and exchanges, such as a competitive voluntary choice of bottled water vs. cheap tap water vs. pumping your own water, may seem relatively benign.

The current battles over depleted water supplies continue to grow intense. But they are not the first such confrontations. In the mid-1800s, when miners and farmers and ranchers all started to fight over precious rivers in western states, the government brought peace by divvying up water so that everyone got what seemed, at the time, to be a fair share. These "usage rights" had the equivalent status of "private property." Farmers couldn't own the water itself, but they could own, and hold title to, the use of a certain defined amount of water, for a certain time, if they met certain conditions.

It was these rights that Mulholland bought up, along with the property, during the infamous secret campaign to drain and divert the Owens River. But as scarcity, competition, a changing climate, and global population growth threaten to deplete waters further, the buying and selling of water rights has become a more transparent, and potentially far more lucrative, multibillion-dollar industry.

Many know T. Boone Pickens as a Texas wildcatter and corporate raider. But in the twenty-first century his interest shifted from oil to alternative energy and in particular to water. After he sank $100 million of his money to buy up farmers' rights to billions of gallons of water, he personally owned more water than any individual on earth. Then he made plans to sell it off to the highest bidder, and in particular, the booming city of Dallas, down a $2.1 billion 654-mile pipeline. "There are people" Pickens said, "who will buy the water when they need it. And the people who have the water want to sell it. That's the blood, guts, and feathers of the thing."

Water depletion has given rise to what may soon become among the biggest businesses on earth. To grasp why this is so, consider the prospects of a potential investor. Supply is shrinking, demand is booming. The customer base (the world's population) is expanding. There are online brokers such as WaterBank.com, iAqua.com, and WaterRightsMarket.com. And for all his rights, Pickens was a small-fry latecomer to the existing private water management giants whose total revenues were projected to reach $1 trillion by 2015. As aquifers dried up, investment brokers gushed. When environmentalists wept at barren rivers, Wall Street analysts smiled at what depletion might do to their water stocks. And where civilians saw loss, portfolio managers saw "an explosive growth business opportunity . . . that presently offers investors a shot at a couple of double-your-money stock ideas" because industry trackers "caught early sight of a major global risk: a burgeoning worldwide water crisis that is now a reality."

Trading water in a market harnesses human greed. But in the process, it also does one thing very well, better than any government. By sending price signals for the value of water at a certain point in time, it leads to highly efficient allocation.

Efficiency can benefit nature. The same legal exchange by which farmers of Owens Valley sold their water rights to Los Angeles (drying up their river) or to a mining company (often polluting the river) is also why today many farmers sell, or lease, their water rights to local fishing groups (to restore trout habitat) and national environmental organizations (to replenish the river).

The thing about markets is that they are not moral. They make no accounting of what the good may be for future generations, only what is expedient today. Also, markets don't care about inequity between rich and poor, just who can pay how much for what. That exposes the risk that by treating water like an absolute commodity, free from the context of social,

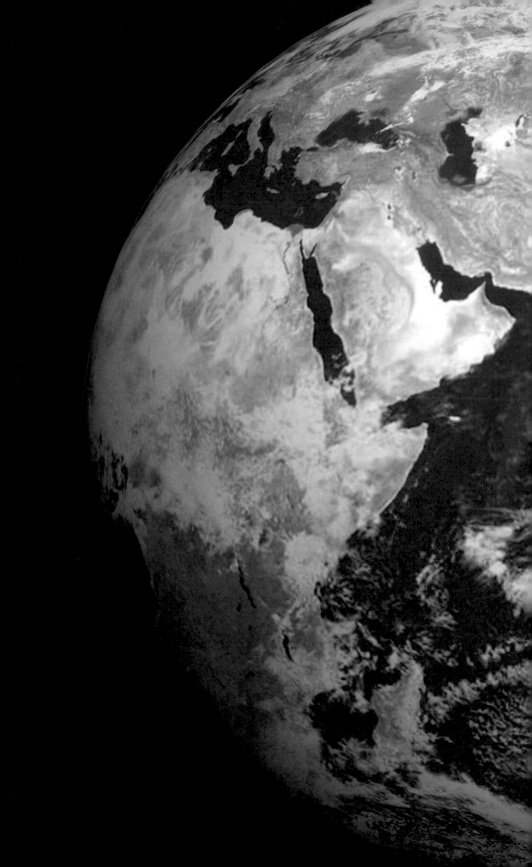

environmental, or even spiritual benefits, a few rich can control the flow of entire rivers. This potential for inequity has always been a concern of every society on earth. But some have managed to cobble together an ethical framework that is fair to all and efficient for nature.

The examples provided by the most ancient and resilient societies of arid landscapes offer lessons from which the world may take some guidance. For starters, every human can indeed be guaranteed a free, daily amount of water.

(continued on page 98)

Water as an ethical good

The morality of trading water is not a new concern. It goes back to the oldest civilizations, and even infuses religious doctrine. "I never remember anything in the Ten Commandments that said making a profit is a sin," said Peter Cook, head of the National Association of Water Companies. "[Selling water] really comes down to a philosophical difference between the municipal sector and the private sector. We believe utilities should be operated as enterprises."

Actually the ancient scriptures do weigh in on that very issue. The Bible condemns those making a profit from water sales: "To the thirsty I will give water without price from the fountain," according to the Book of Revelations 21:6. And the Koran, whose religious doctrine was founded in and spread through an extremely water-scarce landscape, also forbade those with wells from charging the poor for access to it. A certain amount was to be free. This code of conduct guided many desert societies from the nomadic Bedouin of the Sahara to the Bushmen of the Kalahari. In these societies, a certain life-line of water was always provided to anyone for free. Beyond that, for economic gains a tribute or exchange was required. ■

can be traded with others, leading not to waste of a common resource but innovative conservation of something each person owns and all increasingly treasure.

The balance of rights and regulation, equity and efficiency, equal and tradable human shares of water, suggests a way forward. In face of chronic water depletion, Southern California, for example, has been humbled, and keeps learning to do more with less.

On December 6, 2006, Los Angeles mayor Antonio
Villaraigosa opened a gate on the state's vast aqueduct system and restored some of the flow his metropolis had glommed
onto decades earlier. Those at the ceremony knew by heart
the words pronounced by William Mulholland that day he
had diverted water to quench the insatiable appetite of his city.
But times had changed. People were growing wise enough to
accept limits and embrace them in ways that could benefit economic growth and nature. Overall depletion continued due to

The once bone-dry banks of the Owens River are flush with new life today, now that water flows unimpeded along sixty-two winding miles.

rising demand, shrinking supply, and climate change, but in the U.S. the average American was using 10 percent less water than he or she did in 1980.

Los Angeles had been especially austere, encouraging families and businesses with financial incentives to waste less in their homes and offices. Overall efficiency was improving. As Mayor Villaraigosa turned the squeaky valve, water gushed toward the long-dry Owens River Valley, back from where it had been stolen, and began the gradual act of replenishing the earth there. As it did, a top Los Angeles water official, H. David Nahai, made an announcement. He offered a "message of friendship and gratitude" to the people of Owens Valley, but Nahai could have been speaking to all the endangered species of aquatic ecosystems, to the lost wetlands, to the Native Americans, and to those who had come before him, including Mulholland. Finally he paused for a moment of recognition, then offered six humble words that might heal the history of water depletion.

"There it is," he said with a smile. "Take it back."

Sources

Chapter Two: Yesterday's Warning Signs

p. 19,   "neere the place . . ." Richard Hakluyt, *The Principal Navigations, Voyages, Traffiques & Discoveries of the English Nation*, ed. Irwin R. Blacker (New York, NY: Viking Press, 1965), 325.

P. 22,   "Earth's only paradise . . . ," Michael Drayton, "To the Virginian Voyage," http://www.luminarium.org/renlit/Virginian.htm.

p. 22,   "the earth bringeth . . ." David B. Quinn and Alison M. Quinn, *The First Colonists* (Raleigh, NC: North Carolina Division of Archives and History, 1982), 8.

p. 22,   "luscious," Drayton, "To the Virginian Voyage."

p. 22,   "like some delicate . . ." Hakluyt, *The Principal Navigations*, 287.

p. 22,   "most gentle . . ." Ibid., 293.

p. 22,   "greene soil on the hills . . ." Ibid., 287.

p. 22,   "the most plentiful . . ." Ibid., 292.

p. 23,   "good hope that some . . ." Ibid., 325.

p. 23,   "was much further . . ." Ibid., 326.

p. 23,   "secret token," Ibid., 327.

p. 25,   "had the barke taken . . ." Ibid., 328.

p. 25,   "The weather grew to . . ." Ibid., 329.

p. 30,   "the most extreme. . ." David W. Stahle, Malcolm K. Cleaveland, Dennis B. Blanton, Matthew D. Therrell, and David A. Gay, "The Lost Colony and Jamestown," *Science* 280, no. 5363 (April 24, 1998), 564.

p. 30,   "which has scarce . . ." Adam Smith, *An Inquiry Into the Nature and Causes of the Wealth of Nations*, ed. Charles J. Bullock (New York: Cosimo, Inc., 2007), 35.

p. 37,   "about to become . . ." Mark Reisner, *Cadillac Desert: The American West and its Disappearing Waters* (New York, NY: Viking, 1986).

p. 37,   "There it is . . ."Associated Press, "LA Gives Back Water to California River," FoxNews.com, December 6, 2006, http://www.foxnews.com/printer_friendly_wires/2006Dec06/0,4675,WaterWars,00.html.

Chapter Three: The Control of Drought

p. 45, "I honestly . . ." Brenda Goodman, "Amid Drought, a Georgian Consumes a Niagara," *New York Times*, November 15, 2007.

p. 48, "We're taking hundreds . . ." Lynn Waddell and Arian Camp-Flores, "Dry—And Getting Drier: the Severe Drought Has Georgians Praying for Rain—and Battling with Their Neighbors," *Newsweek*, November 16, 2007.

p. 50, "We've come together . . ." Ibid.

p. 64, "There's a two-thirds chance . . ." John Gertner, "The Future is Drying Up," *NewYork Times*, October 21, 2007.

Chapter Four: Tomorrow's Potential Outcomes

p. 79, "Desalination is not . . ." Maude Barlow, *Blue Covenant: The Global Water Crisis and the Coming Battle for the Right to Water* (Toronto, Ontario: McClelland & Stewart Ltd, 2007), 28.

Chapter Five: Regulating Demand and Trading Water

p. 84, "[Bottled water] has a higher . . ." Robert Jerome
Glennon, *Water Follies: Groundwater Pumping and the Fate
of America's Fresh Waters* (Washington, DC: Island Press, 2004), 2.

p. 85, "The Earth's fresh water . . ." Maude Barlow and Tony Clarke,
*Blue Gold: The Fight to Stop the Corporate Theft of the
World's Water* (New York: The New Press, 2002), xvii.

p. 87, "if the primary avenue . . ." Ibid., 121.

p. 87, "Basically we see water . . ." Barlow and Clarke,
Blue Gold, 239.

p. 87, "it raises a number . . ." Environment News Service, "Access
to Water: A Human Right or a Human Need?,"
http://www.ens-newswire.com/ens/mar2009/2009-03-27-03.asp.

p. 89, "There are people . . ." Susan Berfield, "There Will Be Water:
T. Boone Pickens Thinks Water Is the New Oil,"
Business Week, June 12 2008.

p. 90, "an explosive growth business . . ." Dan Dorfman,
"Thirsting for Water Stocks," *New York Sun*, June 20, 2007.

p. 97, "I never remember . . ." Alan Snitnow, Deborah Kaufman, and
Michael Fox, *Thirst: Fighting the Corporate Theft of Our
Water* (New York: John Wiley & Sons, 2007), 11.

p. 100, "message of friendship . . ." Associated Press, "LA Gives Back
Water to California River," FoxNews.com, December 6, 2006.

p. 100, "There it is . . ." Associated Press, "LA Gives Back Water to
California River."

Bibliography

Anderson, Terry L., and Pamela Snyder. *Water Markets: Priming the Invisible Pump*. Washington, DC: Cato Institute, 1997.

Annin, Peter. *The Great Lakes Water Wars*. Washington, DC: Island Press, 2006.

Ball, Philip. *Life's Matrix: A Biography of Water*. New York: Farrar, Straus and Giroux, 1999.

Barlow, Maude. *Blue Covenant: The Global Water Crisis and the Coming Battle for the Right to Water*. New York: New Press, 2007.

Barlow, Maude, and Tony Clark. *Blue Gold: The Fight to Stop the Corporate Theft of the World's Water*. New York: New Press, 2002.

Barringer, Felicity. "Lake Mead Could Be Within a Few Years of Going Dry, Study Says." *New York Times*, February 13, 2008.

Bate, Roger. *The Cost of Free Water: The Global Problem of Water Misallocation and the Case of South Africa*. Johannesburg: Free Market Foundation, 1999.

Borenstein, Seth. "U.S. In For Perilous Weather as World Warms, NASA Says." Associated Press, August 31, 2007.

Brown, Lester R. *Plan B 2.0: Rescuing a Planet Under Stress and a Civilization in Trouble*. New York: Norton, 2006.

Cooley, Heather, Peter Gleick, and Gary Wolf. *Desalination, with a Grain of Salt: A California Perspective*. Oakland, CA: Pacific Institute, 2006.

Cook, Edward R. et al. "North American drought: Reconstructions, Causes, and Consequences." *Earth-Science Reviews* 81, 2007.

Davies, Bryan, and Jenny Day. *Vanishing Waters*. Cape Town: University of Cape Town Press, 1998.

De Villiers, Marq. *Water: The Fate of Our Most Precious Resource*. New York: Houghton Mifflin, 2000.

Diamond, Jared. *Collapse: How Societies Choose to Fail or Succeed*. New York: Viking, 2005.

Fagan, Brian. *The Great Warming: Climate Change and the Rise and Fall of Civilizations*. New York: Bloomsbury, 2008.

Faruqui, Naser I., Askit K. Biswas, and Murad J.Bino, eds. *Water Management in Islam: Water Resources Management and Policy*. New York: United Nations University, 2001.

Finnegan, William. "Leasing the Rain: The World Is Running Out of Fresh Water, and the Fight to Control It Has Begun." *New Yorker*, April 8, 2002.

Flannery, Tim. *The Weather Makers: The History and Future Impact of Climate Change*. New York: Penguin, 2005.

Freid, Stephanie. "Future of War Will Go with the Flow: Water Promises to be a Flash Point." *San Francisco Chronicle*, June 10, 2007.

Gleick, Peter H. *Dirty Water*. New York: Island Press, 1996

——. "Making Every Drop Count." *Scientific American*, February 2001.

——. *The World's Water: The Biennial Report on Fresh Wate Resouces, 2002-2003*. Washington, DC: Island Press, 2002.

Gleick, Peter H., Gary Wolff, Elizabeth L. Chalecki, and Rachel Reyes. *The New Economy of Water: The Risks and Benefits of Globalization and Privatization of Fresh Water.* Oakland: Pacific Institute, 2002.

Glennon, Robert. *Water Follies: Groundwater Pumping and the Fate of America's Fresh Waters.* Washington, DC: Island Press, 2002.

Hall, David. "Water in Public Hands: Public Sector Water Management—A Necessary Option." *Public Services International,* June 2001.

Hamner, Jesse H., and Aaron T. Wolf, "Patterns in International Water Resource Treatises: The Transboundary Freshwater Dispute Database." *Colorado Journal of International Law and Policy,* 1997.

Hunt, Constance Elizabeth. *Thirsty Planet: Strategies for Sustainable Water Management.* New York: Zed Books, 2004.

Integrated Regional Information Networks: In-Depth. *Running Dry: The Humanitarian Impact of the Global Water Crisis.* New York: UN, October 2006.

Intergovernmental Panel on Climate Change. *Climate Change, 2001. Contributions of Working Groups I, II, and III to the Third Assessment Report of the Intergovernmental Panel on Climate Change.* New York: Cambridge University Press. 2001.

International Consortium of Investigative Journalists. Edited by M. Beelman et al. *The Water Barons: How a Few Private Water Companies are Privatizing Your Water.* Washington, DC: Public Integrity Books, 2003.

International Rivers Network. "Spreading the Water Wealth: Making Water Infrastructure Work for the Poor." *Dams Rivers & People: IRN,* 2006.

Jehl, Douglas. *Whose Water Is It?: The Unquenchable Thirst of a Water-Hungry World.* Washington, DC: National Geographic, 2003.

Khagram, Sanjeev. *Dams and Development: Transnational Struggles for Water and Power.* Ithaca, NY: Cornell University Press, 2004.

Koeppel, Gerald T. *Water for Gotham: A History.* Princeton, NJ: Princeton University Press, 2000.

Lagod, Martin "We're Running Out of Water." *San Francisco Chronicle,* July 8, 2007.

Lavelle, Marianne. "Why You Should Worry About Water: How This Diminishing Resource Will Determine the Future of Where and How We Live." *US News & World Report,* June 4, 2007.

Leslie, Jacques. *Deep Water: The Epic Struggle over Dams, Displaced People, and the Environment.* New York: Farrar, Straus and Giroux, 2005.

——. "Running Dry: What Happens When the World No Longer Has Enough Freshwater?" *Harpers,* July 2000.

Lomborg, Bjorn. *The Skeptical Environmentalist: Measuring the Real State of the World. Cambridge:* Cambridge University Press, 2001.

Mann, Charles. "The Rise of Big Water." *Vanity Fair,* May 2007.

Martin, Glen. "Water Woes: Projecting 60 years into California's thirsty future."

San Francisco Chronicle Magazine, January 7, 2007.

McCully, Patrick. *Silenced Rivers: The Ecology and Politics of Large Dams.* London: Zed Books, 2001.

Midkiff, Ken. *Not a Drop to Drink: America's Water Crisis (And What You Can Do).* New York: New World Library, 2007.

Millennium Ecosystem Assessment. *Ecosystems and Human Well-Being: Synthesis.* Washington, DC: Island Press, 2005.

Miller, Lee. *Roanoke: Solving the Mystery of the Lost Colony.* New York: Penguin Books, 2000.

Molden, David, Charlotte De Fraiture, and Frank Rijsberman. "Water Scarcity: The Food Factor," *Issues in Science and Technology*, Summer 2007.

Montaigne, Fen. "Water Pressure: The Earth's Six Billion People Already Overtax Its Supply of Accessible Fresh Water. What Happens When the Planet Gets a Few Billion More Hands?" *National Geographic*, August 2003.

NASA, Goddard Institute for Space Studies. *Surface Temperature Analysis.* Data. giss.nasa.gov/gistemp.

O'Driscoll, Patrick. "A Drought for the Ages." *USA Today*, June 8, 2007.

Pearce, Fred. *When the Rivers Run Dry: Water—the Defining Crisis of the Twenty-First Century.* Boston: Beacon Press, 2006.

Peet, John. "Priceless: A Survey of Water." *Economist*, July 19, 2003.

Postel, Sandra. *Last Oasis: Facing Water Scarcity.* New York: W. W. Norton, 1997.

———. *Pillar of Sand: Can the Irrigation Miracle Last?* New York: W. W. Norton, 1999.

Powell, James Lawrence. *Dead Pool: Lake Powell, Global Warming, and the Future of Water in the West.* Berkeley: University of California Press, 2009.

Rothfelder, Jeffrey. *Every Drop for Sale: Our Desperate Battle over Water in a World About to Run Out.* New York: Penguin Putnam, 2001.

Royte, Elizabeth. *Bottlemania: How Water Went on Sale and Why We Bought It.* New York: Bloomsbury, 2008.

Saleth, R. Maria, and Ariel Dinar. *The Institutional Economics of Water: A Cross-Country Analysis of Institutions and Performance.* Washington, DC: IBRD/World Bank, 2004.

Saltzman, James. *Thirst: A Short History of Drinking Water.* Raleigh, NC: Duke Law School Faculty Scholarship Series, 2006.

Scully, Malcolm G. "The Politics of Running Out of Water." *Chronicle of Higher Education*, November 17, 2000.

Shiva, Vandana. *Water Wars: Privatization, Pollution, and Profit.* Cambridge: South End Press, 2002.

Simon, Paul (senator). *Tapped Out: The Coming World Crisis in Water and What We Can Do About It.* New York: Welcome Rain, 1998.

SIWI, IUCN, IWMI, IFPRI. *Let It Reign: The New Water Paradigm for Global Food Security.* Working Report to the Commission on Sustainable Development-13, Stockholm International Water Institute, 2004.

Smith, Adam. *An Inquiry into the Nature and Causes of the Wealth of Nations.* Chicago: University of Chicago Press, 1976.

Snitow, Alan, Deborah Kaufman, and Michael Fox. *Thirst: Fighting the Corporate Theft of Our Water.* New York: John Wiley & Sons, 2007.

Specter, Michael. "The Last Drop: Confronting The Possibility of a Global

Catastrophe." *New Yorker*, October 23, 2006.

Speth, James Gustave. *Red Sky at Morning: America and the Crisis of the Global Environment.* New Haven, CT: Yale University Press, 2005.

Stahle, David W. et al "The Lost Colony and Jamestown Droughts." *Science* 280, no. 564 (1998).

Stegner, Wallace. *Beyond the 100th Meridian.* New York: Penguin, 1992.

Steinhauer, Jennifer. "Water Starved California Slows Development; Law Requires 20-Year Supply." *New York Times*, June 7, 2008.

Tagliabue, John. "As Multinationals Run the Taps, Anger Rises Over Water for Profit," *New York Times*, August 26, 2002.

Tzu, Sun. *The Art of War.* Translated from the Chinese by Thomas Leay. Boston: Shambhala, 1988.

UNDP. *Beyond Scarcity: Power, Poverty and the Global Water Crisis.* Summary of the Human Development Report, 2006.

Vidal, John. "Australia suffers worst drought in 1000 years: Depleted reservoirs, failed crops and arid farmland spark global warming tussle." *Guardian* (London), November 8, 2006.

Ward, Diane Raines. *Water Wars: Drought, Floods, Folly and the Politics of Thirst.* New York: Riverhead Books, 2002.

White, John. "Return To Ronoake" (1590). In Richard Hakluyt, *Principal Navigations, Voyages of the English Nation, vol. III.* London, 1600.

Wolf, Aaron T. "Conflict and Cooperation along International Waterways." *Water Policy* 1, no. 2 (1998).

Wolff, G., and E. Hallstein. *Beyond Privatization: Restructuring Water Systems to Improve Performance.* Oakland, CA: Pacific Institute, 2005.

Wood, Chris. *Dry Spring: The Coming Water Crisis of North America.* Vancouver, BC: Raincoast Books, 2008.

World Commission on Dams. *Dams and Development: A New Framework for Decision-Making.* London: Earthscan, 2000.

Workman, James G. "How to Fix Our Dam Problems." *Issues in Science and Technology*, Fall 2007.

Worster, Donald. *Rivers of Empire: Water, Aridity, and the Growth of the American West.* New York: Oxford University Press, 1985.

Zito, Kelly. "Dry Spell Danger: Skimpy Snowpack, Low Rainfall, Growing Populations and Demands of Agriculture and Recreation Add Up to an Urgent Need for Water Conservation as Californians Stare into the Face of drought." *San Francisco Chronicle*, May 2, 2008.

Web Sites

U.S. Geological Survey's Water Science for Schools
http://ga.water.usgs.gov/edu/index.htm

Water Resources of the United States
http://water.usgs.gov

World Health Organization's "10 Facts About Water Scarcity"
http://who.int/features/factfiles/water/en/index.htm

UN Water: Resouces for Children and Young People
http:www.unwater.org/kids.html

The Online NewsHour Extra: Water Fights Present Dangerous Challenges in Coming Decades
http://www.pbs.org/newshour/extra/features/world/jan-june09/water_03-20.html

U.S. Drought Portal
http://www.drought.gov

Photo Credits

16-17, 20-21, 24: **North Wind Picture Archives/Alamy**; 38, 39: **Private Collection**: 59: **U.S. Department of Energy**; 86: Maude Barlow and the Council of Canadians; all other images used under license from **Shutterstock, Inc**.

Index

A

B

C

D

E

F

G